QUESTIONS: BUDDHISTS

If you wish to untie a knot, you must first understand how it was tied.

Surangama Sutra

We can only change the world if we change our way of thinking. We must practise finding ourselves in the present moment, not carried away by worries and fears.

Thich Nhat Hanh

Buddhism is often taught in schools, but it is not often that there is much time to go beyond presenting key teachings (such as the Three Marks of existence or the Four Noble Truths) and key actions (such as the Eightfold Path and the Five Precepts).

In this book, we have tried to cover some of these fundamental Buddhist tenets, while seeing that Buddhism is a path rather than a set of beliefs, and that there is real diversity of paths to follow within Buddhism. We have included the words of Buddhists from the Theravada and Mahayana traditions, including Tibetan Buddhism, the Thai Forest Sangha, Soto Zen and the Triratna Buddhist Order.

We offer students the chance to begin to understand how Buddhism says that the knot of existence is tied, in reference to the Surangama Sutra quotation on this page, as well as how it may be untied (pp.5-10, 17-24). We point students towards the kind of Engaged Buddhism espoused by Thich Nhat Hanh and others. We also take the example of Aung San Suu Kyi's fight for freedom and justice in Burma (pp.25-30).

There is currently a great deal of interest in the benefits of meditation, and particularly in learning from great Buddhist practitioners – hence the strong links between the Dalai Lama and neuroscientists through his Mind and Life Institute. Pages 11-16 explore the importance of meditation within Buddhism while allowing students to taste some meditative experiences.

In RE we want to enable students to understand something of the power and impact for followers of a religious path. However, we also want this exploration to illuminate their own path, challenging them to deep thinking about the knot of life and how it may be untied.

Stephen Pett
Editor

Note:

Buddhist terms in this book are given in both Sanskrit and Pali. Given the diversity of Buddhist traditions covered, there is not total uniformity of terms. In general, Sanskrit spellings are given first, with Pali in brackets: for example, karma (P. kamma). Where contributions occur from members of the Theravada tradition, the Pali spelling is given first, followed by the Sanskrit; for example, Dhamma (S. Dharma).

Contents

A VIEW FROM INSIDE BUDDHISM

It is always important for students of RE to hear authentic voices from inside in a faith community. Dr Joyce Miller, formerly an RE teacher and adviser, belongs to the Thai Forest Sangha, a tradition within Theravada Buddhism. We asked her to bring together her Buddhist and teacher identities and answer some questions about teaching Buddhism. (*Note:* In accordance with the Theravada School, we have used the Pali terms in this article.)

Dr Joyce Miller

What do you want young people to know about Buddhism in Britain today?

That Buddhism is a spiritual, moral and religious practice that has worldwide significance. I want young people to understand the key aspects of the Buddha's teaching and that they provide a coherent analysis of the situation in which we live and a means of achieving happiness and wellbeing within it.

What matters most in British Buddhism at the moment? Why?

I think there are two answers to this. The first is that I don't feel that I am part of 'British Buddhism' – I'm not sure what that is. I am a Buddhist living in Britain, trying to follow the Buddha's teaching. We're not evangelical and we don't have a strong socio-political agenda to pursue. Buddhists aren't much into labels.

It's also true, however, to say that the practice of compassion is extremely important and therefore there is deep concern about issues of social justice and suffering. Many Buddhists in Britain will identify with Buddhist countries where there are major political problems, such as Burma and Tibet.

There are issues, for some Buddhists, about the place of women and the perceived inferior status of nuns as opposed to monks, but I try not to get caught up in these controversies. Buddhism is an ancient, eastern religion that is adapting to life in the West and this is a long, gradual process. It's also important to find a balance between our Western perspectives and what the Buddha taught was the real path to finding wellbeing. There are tensions there that we need to continue to try to resolve and that will take time and patience.

What are the questions that Buddhists worry about? What are the issues that concern the Buddhist community?

Do we worry? My teacher often talks about not turning a difficulty into a problem. The reality is that life is unsatisfactory and we try to remember to face difficulties in the knowledge of the first Noble Truth. That doesn't mean that we don't get involved in issues, but we try to keep a balanced perspective on all such questions.

There are issues that are of concern to Buddhists – the environment or human rights, for example – and I would guess that many will give support to charities that work in areas they are concerned about – but it's important to remember that Buddhism is the middle path and it's always about striving for equanimity, as well as practising compassion and kindness. Non-attachment is difficult but it's partly about not getting too emotionally caught up in issues, however noble they might be.

RE Today Services

What are your favourite stories and sayings of the Buddha?

In the tradition to which I belong, the focus is on meditation and morality rather than stories and texts. The Buddha's teachings underpin all of this but rarely do we read the scriptures, as such. On the full and new moon days, each month, the abbot of the monastery I support sends out, by email, a quotation from the *Dhammapada*, a collection of very beautiful, short Buddhist teachings and to this he adds his own commentary on how it can help us on our spiritual path. The *Dhammapada* is very accessible and, I think, inspirational.

My other favourite is the teachings on the divine abidings, the Brahmaviharas, which are about the cultivation of four key qualities: kindness (metta), compassion (karuna), sympathetic joy (mudita) and equanimity (upekkha). I often use these as the basis for meditation and reflection and hope they help me develop those qualities.

What issues do you want RE teachers to remember when they plan to teach about Buddhism?

That Buddhism is more than a philosophy of life. It's easy to secularise Buddhism and I think one of the reasons it is so popular in the West is that it doesn't make demands in terms of what one believes. But it is a religion with rituals, teachings, a strong ethical code and a body of literature. Teaching Buddhism offers a real opportunity to explore some fundamental questions about our lives and to develop pupils' conceptual understanding.

What else would you like to say?

I'm about to commit heresy and say that I don't think pupils below A level need to learn about, for example, the differences between Theravada and Mahayana Buddhism or that they need to study a variety of traditions. Focusing on the Buddha's teaching and how that is interpreted in people's lives is sufficient at school level.

These pages were written for teachers but you might get your older students to use them and ask them to:

- identify what is most important to Joyce, giving evidence
- find two statements that make them think and explain why
- devise some more questions they would like to put to Joyce
- contact a Buddhist from a different tradition and ask the same questions; can they explain the reasons for any differences?

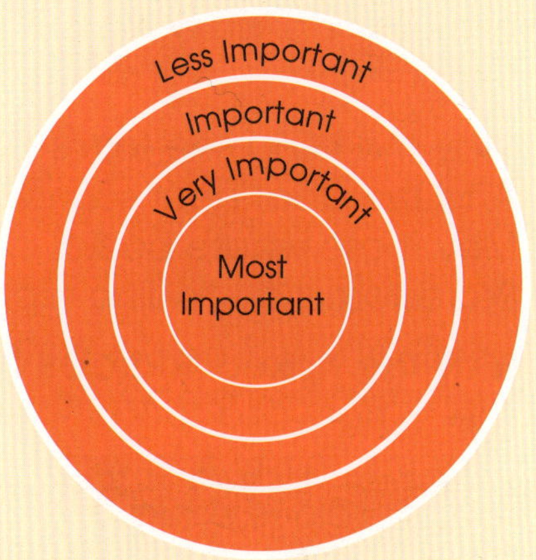

Learning from Buddhist ways of living

1 After reading Joyce Miller's answers carefully, ask students to work in pairs or individually to try and identify **nine** key words that sum up what Buddhism means to her.

2 Compare their nine words with this selection. Note any words that match their own choices, and any different words chosen. Decide together which are the best nine words from this list and their own.

The Buddha	Kindness	Compassion
Happiness	Equanimity	Non-attachment
Meditation	Morality	Rituals

3 Use the nine words agreed in the pairs, plus a selection of other words suggested in Activity 2 (between 5 and 10). Use a target board and ask students to go through the words one at a time, deciding where to place them on the target board. They should place one word in the centre, and then 3, 5 and 7 words as the rings move away from the centre. The rings represent what is of ultimate importance to Buddhists (from this interview); what is very important; quite important; not so important. Use this again after some further study of Buddhism, adding key words and concepts to assess your students' understanding. There will be no single right answer to this.

4 Ask students for their own suggestions for how we find happiness in the situation in which we live.

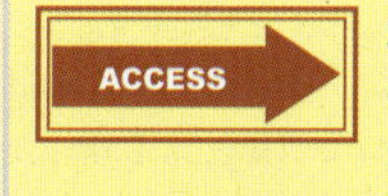

See p.31 for an activity to make this more accessible to lower-achieving students.

May all beings everywhere . . .

This prayer of dedication is a compliation of verses by Shantideva, a Buddhist master from India in the eighth century CE. It is from the **Bodhicaryavatara**, or **A Guide to the Bodhissatva's Way of Life**. It is one of His Holiness the Dalai Lama's favourite prayers, and is important to many Buddhists, particularly those from the Tibetan traditions.

May all beings everywhere
Plagued by sufferings of body and mind
Obtain an ocean of happiness and joy
By virtue of my merits.

May no living creature suffer,
Commit evil, or ever fall ill.
May no one be afraid or belittled,
With a mind weighed down by
  depression.

May the blind see forms
And the deaf hear sounds,
May those whose bodies are worn with toil
Be restored on finding repose.

May the naked find clothing,
The hungry find food;
May the thirsty find water
And delicious drinks.

May the poor find wealth,
Those weak with sorrow find joy;
May the forlorn find hope,
Constant happiness, and prosperity.

May there be timely rains
And bountiful harvests;
May all medicines be effective
And wholesome prayers bear fruit.

May all who are sick and ill
Quickly be freed from their ailments.
Whatever diseases there are in the world,
May they never occur again.

May the frightened cease to be afraid
And those bound be freed;
May the powerless find power,
And may people think of benefiting
  each other.

For as long as space remains,
For as long as sentient beings remain,
Until then may I too remain
To dispel the miseries of the world.

Seven ways to use Shantideva's prayer

1 Read the Dedication aloud. What tone is best? What difference does it make if you read it calmly or enthusiastically, grumpily or angrily, fast or slowly?

2 Get students working in groups. Half of the groups should list words that describe the world as it is expressed in the prayer; the other half should list words describing the world as Shantideva would like it to be. They can use words in the poem as well as their own words.

3 Give each verse to a group of three or four students. Ask them to come up with a freeze-frame or a short drama to express something from *before* the prayer, and one to express what might happen if the prayer is fulfilled.

4 Give each student in the class one line or couplet to express through art or sculpture. They should consider an appropriate colour to express the emotion of the phrase, as well as images or symbols to express the meaning and the hope. Create a display using all of the artwork alongside the prayer.

5 The Buddha taught that his followers should practise *metta* (P.metta) – loving-kindness to all beings. Using the information in this prayer, ask students to come up with a definition of metta, with examples to show what it means in action.

6 Set students the task of finding an example of this prayer being fulfilled in the news during the next week. Get them to bring in the information and to be able to describe the people or individuals who have brought the good news into reality. Have students themselves done anything to help?

7 Ask students to imagine they were to recite this Dedication every day. What difference might it make to how they live? Give three things they probably would not do any more and three things they probably would do.

WHAT IS THE HEART OF BUDDHIST TEACHING? DOES IT MATTER?

Summary of learning

The essence of the Buddha's teaching on the causes of suffering and the way to end suffering, is expressed in the Four Noble Truths. The fourth Noble Truth is also known as the Eightfold Path.

Written for **students aged 11–12,** the activities in this section are designed to introduce students to the Buddha's teaching in a variety of active ways which encourage them to reflect on their own understandings and questions about the causes of suffering and the things that give their life value and purpose.

Resources

BBC's Learning Zone Broadband Clips Library

A searchable database of video clips on a variety of topics covered in RE, e.g. clips 8349-8350

See: www.bbc.co.uk/learningzone/clips

Buddhanet

An extensive site on many aspects of Buddhism including a story of the life of the Buddha, an interactive Wheel of Life and a collection of Buddhist stories.

See: www.buddhanet.net/e-learning/
buddhism/lifebuddha

CLEO

A collection of short videos designed for the RE classroom including an interactive Wheel of Life with commentary and template to design your own Wheel of Life. Choose KS3 section.

See: www.cleo.net.uk

The Dhammapada

An illustrated version of the Dhammapada:

See: www.buddhanet.net
dhammapada/index.htm

Using the pages

Activity 1 Three wishes

This activity is designed to open up discussion about desire and craving as an introduction to the Four Noble Truths. It is useful to return to this activity following Activity 2 and ask students to reflect on any fresh insights and questions they may have.

Activity 2 The Four Sights

This activity uses simple drama and digital cameras to engage students with the impact of the Four Sights on the development of Siddhartha Gautama's thinking and teaching (P. Siddhattha Gotama).

Activity 3 The Parable of the Arrow

The Parable of the Arrow introduces the idea that the Buddha had made a diagnosis of the human condition and identified a cure, and a prescription to follow for the cure. It explains why the Buddha did not offer comment on speculative questions.

Activity 4 Ethical conduct

Students will need a response sheet (p.10) and a set of cards (pp. 8–9) for each group. The activity asks them to consider: the meaning of ethical conduct as expressed in some Buddhist texts; how some Buddhists express this in action; how students' own actions reflect their beliefs.

A version of the life of the Buddha for Activity 2 on p.6 is also available as a downloadable presentation available for subscribers.

See p.31 for a version of Activity 1 suited to lower-achieving students.

Suggestions for higher-achieving students can be found on p.32.

Outcomes

Students can demonstrate achievement at levels 4–6 in these activities if they can say 'yes' to some of these 'I can' statements:

Description of achievement:
I can . . .

Level 4

- describe and link up Buddhist beliefs about ethical conduct and how Buddhists show this in their behaviour
- ask questions and suggest some answers about why Buddhists try to live ethically.

Level 5

- explain the impact for Buddhists of believing that there is a 'cure' for suffering
- connect my own views about causes and cures of suffering with the understandings expressed by Buddhists.

Level 6

- interpret Buddhist texts and use examples to give an informed account of what Buddhists mean by the Four Noble Truths
- express my own insights into the understanding of the causes and cure for suffering offered by Buddhism.

For the teacher

Where two spellings are given for key Buddhist terms, the first is in Sanskrit, with the Pali following in brackets e.g. karma (kamma) and duhkha (dukkha). Sanskrit is the language of the texts of the Mahayana school, while Pali is used in the Theravada school.

"

Introducing the Four Noble Truths

Activity 1 Three wishes

Explain to students that this activity gives them a chance to think about their hopes and dreams, what they are and how likely they are to come true. This will provide a perspective from which to approach the meaning of the Four Noble Truths.

Ask students to:

1 **Imagine** they have been granted three wishes. They can ask for anything they like (other than asking for more wishes!). Prompt them to think carefully, and then write down their wishes.

2 **Think about** how likely, under normal circumstances, it is that their wishes will come true, rating each wish as follows:

1 = very likely; 2 = quite likely; 3 = unlikely; 4 = very unlikely.

This encourages students to think about **how realistic** their wishes are.

3 **Think about** who the wishes benefit, rating each wish as follows:

A = very unselfish; B = fairly unselfish; C = quite selfish; D = very selfish.

This encourages students to think about the **nature** of their wishes.

4 In small groups or as a class, **talk about** how they understand questions e.g.

o What are the 'basic needs' for living?

o What is the difference between 'needs' and 'wants'?

o Does happiness depend on having all you 'need' or 'want'?

o Is greed or craving ever a good thing? Use Resource 1 (p.7) as a stimulus. What examples of human greed can students suggest?

o Is there a way of achieving happiness in life? What is it and why do they think that?

5 **Introduce** students to the Four Noble Truths. Their discussion will have touched on what Buddhists understand by the concept of Duhkha (P. Dukkha). Can they see connections between their discussion and the Four Noble Truths? How was their thinking similar and different?

Note: when students have completed Activity 2 on p.7 on the Four Sights it would be useful for them to revisit this activity – answering as they think the Buddha might have responded:

a before the experience

b afterwards.

Activity 2 The Four Sights

Introduce students to the Four Sights as a turning point, or spiritual crisis, in the life of Siddartha Gautama (P. Siddhattha Gotama) as he searched for the answer to the question of why people suffer. Some Buddhists consider the literal accuracy of the account to be important, while others 'sit light' with this and regard it as more of a reflection of Siddhartha's spiritual journey away from a life of privilege to the life of a holy man.

1 **Make available** an account of the Four Sights. There are video and text-based versions available online e.g. Clip 3782 on BBC's Learning Zone Clips Library and Buddhanet's 'The Life of the Buddha'.

2 Working in groups of 4 or 5 students **break the story down** into a small number of key moments – creating a storyboard.

3 Students use a digital camera to **photograph** members of their group in key scenes in the story. They **import** the pictures into presentation software, **adding** well-thought-out speech and thought bubbles.

4 They **compare** their work with that of another group and **improve** their presentation in light of the feedback.

5 Students then **write a commentary** on the process: what did they do? Learn? Find hard? Enjoy? How would they do this differently in the future? What advice would they give to a group starting this next? How did they manage to catch the spiritual emphasis of the story?

6 Groups **reflect** on the question 'Was Siddhartha right to leave his wife and family to pursue his own questions about suffering?' and share their thoughts with the class.

Activity 3 The Parable of the Arrow

Siddhartha Gautama came to understand the nature of the existential condition for all beings, and how suffering or 'dis-ease' lies at the heart of it (the first three of the Four Noble Truths). His teachings offered a 'prescription' or 'remedy' for the 'dis-ease'.

The Parable of the Arrow expresses Siddhartha's thinking.

Ask students to **read** the parable (see Resource 3 on p.7) – and **identify** what the Buddha is saying about:

- the relationship between disease, diagnosis, prescription and cure – and the human condition. Do they agree or disagree? What questions does it raise for them?

- the value of speculation about 'big questions' which do not relate directly to the human condition. Do they agree or disagree? What questions does it raise for them?

Resource 1 How to catch a monkey

A popular story tells of the best way to catch a monkey.

o First, find a coconut shell and cut a hole in it. The hole needs to be just large enough for a monkey to fit its hand in.

o Next, attach the coconut shell to a tree or rock, so that it cannot be tipped up or removed.

o Place a tasty piece of fruit inside the shell.

o The monkey reaches inside the shell and grasps the fruit. But when it tries to take the fruit out, its hand is too large for the hole!

o If the monkey clings to the fruit, it cannot remove its hand and is stuck there when the hunter arrives.

o If the monkey lets go of the fruit, it can escape.

Resource 2 The Four Noble Truths

The Four Noble Truths were set out in the Buddha's first sermon.

1 **Duhkha (dukkha)** – dis-ease, unsatisfactoriness, imperfection, suffering (The illness)

2 **Samudaya** – craving (tanha or trishna) and ignorance, the origins of duhkha (The cause of the illness)

3 **Nirodha** – the cessation of duhkha, Nirvana (Nibbana) (The cure)

4 **Marga (Magga)** – the path leading to the cessation of duhkha, the Middle Way (The prescription).

The Four Noble Truths are fundamental to all Buddhist teachings; it is from these that all else follows. They are to be understood as a whole. The first three analyse the human condition, likening it to an illness, and the fourth affirms the remedy.

Resource 3 The Parable of the Arrow

The Buddha was sitting in the park when his disciple Malunkyaputta approached him. Malunkyaputta was bothered that the Buddha had not explained many things, e.g. Is the world eternal or not eternal? Is the soul different to the body? If he did not find answers to these questions he was thinking of leaving the religious life altogether.

The Buddha replied in this way. Suppose a man is wounded by an arrow smeared with poison and his friends and relatives take him to a doctor. Suppose the man then said that he would not have the arrow taken out until he had got the answers to a host of questions such as who had shot him, what caste the person was from, what his name was, whether he was tall, short or of medium stature, what colour complexion he has, what town or city he comes from, what kind of bow was used, what sort of feather was used and what sort of material the point of the arrow was made of.

Malunkyaputta said that surely the man would die if he was to wait until all these questions were answered before the arrow was removed.

The Buddha replied that there were many things he had not explained, because they were speculations and were not useful to the spiritual life. However, those things that he had explained, expressed in the Four Noble Truths, were the things that Malunkyaputta needed to know and understand, for these were the things that would lead to Enlightenment.

What do Buddhist texts say about Ethical Conduct?

1

The Eightfold Path

The Eightfold Path is the **Middle Way** which is the fourth of the **Four Noble Truths** – the means through which **duhkha (P.dukkha)** can be ended. It is divided into three aspects of Buddhist practice:

- **Wisdom**
  - Right View
  - Right Intention
- **Ethical Conduct**
  - Right Speech
  - Right Action
  - Right Livelihood
- **Mental Discipline**
  - Right Effort
  - Right Mindfulness
  - Right Concentration

Cards 2–16 focus on Ethical Conduct – however, you will see that they overlap with Wisdom and Mental Discipline. Why do you think this is?

2

Good people keep going whatever happens. They don't chatter pointlessly. They are the same whether touched by happiness or sorrow.

If a person wishes neither for a child, nor for wealth, nor for power, nor for success by unfair means, then that person is good, wise, and virtuous.

Dhammapada 83 – 84,

3

And what, friends, is the unwholesome? . . . Killing living beings . . . taking what is not given . . . misconduct in sensual pleasures . . . false speech . . . malicious speech . . . harsh speech . . . gossip . . . covetousness . . . wrong view . . .

And what is the root of the unwholesome? Greed . . . hate . . . delusion.

Sammaditthi Sutta, 4, 5
(Access to Insight)

4

Better it would be to swallow a heated iron ball, like flaring fire, than that a bad unrestrained person should live on the alms on the people.

An act carelessly performed, a broken vow, and hesitating obedience to discipline, all this brings no great reward.

Dhammapada 307, 312 (Muller translation 1881)

5

The thoughtless man may be able to recite the law, but if he does not act on it, he has none of the benefits of a life of contemplation. He is like a cowherd counting the cows of others.

The one who acts on the law – even if he can only recite a small part of it – having forsaken passion and hatred and foolishness, possesses true knowledge and calmness of mind. Not clinging to this world or the world to come, he has the benefits of a life of contemplation.

Dhammapada 19 – 20

6

To avoid all evil, to cultivate good, and to cleanse one's mind — this is the teaching of the Buddhas.

Dhammapada 183 (Access to Insight)

7

One who destroys life, utters lies, takes what is not given, goes to another man's wife, and is addicted to intoxicating drinks — such a man digs up his own root even in this world.

Dhammapada 246 (Access to Insight)

8

Whoever steals what is considered to belong to others, whether it be situated in villages or in the forest . . . Whoever having contracted debts defaults when asks to pay, retorts 'I am not indebted to you' . . . Whoever is desirous of stealing even a trifle and kills a person going along the road in order to take it . . . he is to be known as an outcast.

Sutta Nipata, 119–21

9

And what, bhikkhus (fully ordained monks), is wrong livelihood? Scheming, talking, hinting, belittling, pursuing gain with gain: this is wrong livelihood.

Mahācāttarisaka Sutta – The Great Forty

RE Today
Services

10

Ethical Conduct

This part of the Eightfold Path is about how Buddhists should behave towards others and their environment.

- **Right Speech**

  Buddhists should avoid telling lies, spreading gossip, using abusive language, promoting division and hostility between people.

  Buddhists should try to speak positively, be sincere, accurate, kind and gentle, speaking in ways which encourage harmony and getting on with others, and remaining silent when there is nothing to say.

- **Right Action**

  Buddhists should aim to follow the Five Precepts:

  o Not to destroy or harm living beings

  o Not to take what is not freely given

  o Not to misuse sex

  o Not to lie

  o Not to use drugs or alcohol.

- **Right Livelihood**

  Buddhists should aim to earn their living in a way that does not go against Buddhist principles. Work should benefit others and should not harm them, e.g. by trading in arms, or alcohol, killing animals or cheating.

11

BUDDHIST MONK PLANS TO BUY BRIGHTON PIER

Kelsang Pawo, a Buddhist monk, set out to raise £500,000 to buy Brighton Pier by auctioning works of art. He wanted to turn it into a symbol of worldwide hope and love.

See: http://bit.ly/GHQS5N

© The Gesar Foundation

12

The **Dharmachakra**, or Wheel of life, is a symbol that represents Dharma (Dhamma), the Buddha's teaching of the path to Enlightenment.

13

The 28th Niwano Peace Prize 2011

The award went to Sulak Sivaraksa, 'whose work for peace is exemplified by courage, determination and the constant inspiration of the core principles of his Buddhist faith. He has promoted Engaged Buddhism to struggle for human and environmental justice. He is a living example of simplicity, loving-kindness, and compassion. Selflessness is at the heart of Sulak's universal vision.'

See: http://bit.ly/l5OfP9

14

On listening

Listening cultivates wisdom and removes ignorance. It is like a torch that dispels ignorance. If you enrich your mental continuum by listening, no one can steal that wealth. It is the supreme wealth.

The Dalai Lama

© iStockphoto LP

15

The Karuna Trust

Since 1980 Karuna has worked closely with members of India's Dalit community, millions of whom live in terrible poverty.

Karuna strives to help oppressed people to develop the skills, dignity and confidence to transform their lives and take their rightful place in society.

See: www.karuna.org

16

Buddhist charity turns bottles into blankets

For three years the Tzu Chi Foundation in Taiwan has been taking plastic bottles from the waste stream of Taipei, a city of 2.6 million, to convert them into about 244,000 polyester blankets intended for disaster zones. It has sent volunteers with relief supplies to some of the world's biggest disasters.

See: http://reut.rs/lbGGsZ

What does Ethical Conduct mean to Buddhists?

The Eightfold Path

	What does it mean?	What are examples of the opposite?	Why did the Buddha think this mattered?	To follow this, what would I need to change?
Right Speech				
Right Action				
Right Livelihood				

WHY DO BUDDHISTS MEDITATE AND WHAT CAN WE LEARN FROM IT?

Summary of learning

Meditation is centrally important to Buddhists. It directly connects with three of the 'spokes' of the Eightfold Path. However, meditation is only part of the path that many Buddhists take on their spiritual journey. It needs to be accompanied by the development of wisdom and morality too.

Written for **students aged 11–14**, the activities in this section are designed to introduce students to the practices that make up meditation. It is not appropriate for students to be doing Buddhist meditation within their RE lessons, but this unit includes some meditative exercises to give students an idea of the kinds of practices involved. They are asked to make a creative response to their experience before analysing and evaluating the impact of meditation for Buddhists.

For the teacher

The three parts of the Eightfold Path that focus on the practice of meditation are:

Right Effort: a conscious attempt to prevent unskilful states of mind and develop wholesome states, e.g. equanimity not anger, contentment not envy.

Right Mindfulness: the development of concentration, so that the meditator is more aware of her/his thoughts and more able to nurture wholesome states of mind.

Right Concentration: deep states of concentration bring equanimity and awareness. This practice helps meditators to concentrate on wholesome thoughts and attitudes, concentrating deeply enough to step away from the mind and grasp the truth of duhkha (dukkha) (unsatisfactoriness), anitya (anicca) (impermanence) and anatman (anatta) (insubstantiality).

Using the pages

Activity 1 Experiencing stillness

Sample scripts are given for leading stilling exercises, p.12. Teachers should ensure that there is an appropriate classroom atmosphere for these exercises, and offer pupils the option to sit quietly, without distracting anyone else, if they do not wish to participate.

Activity 2 Expressing insight

Ask students to express their experiences creatively by writing a haiku, a simple but effective structure.

Activity 3 Exploring Buddhist meditation

Students use the information from Buddhist sources on p.15 to explore the nature and impact of meditation. Copy p.15 and cut up sets of cards for pairs of students. They can express this creatively through some artwork, using the template on p.16 as a starting point.

A preparatory activity for lower-achieving students can be found on p.31.

Taking it further:

Activity 4 Evaluating

For more able students a further question could be considered:

Should non-Buddhists practise Buddhist meditation?

This could be answered with a written balanced or persuasive argument or explored through discussion.

It could explore ideas such as whether you can take the religion out of a practice; whether the practice of meditation should be open to all because of its beneficial impact on people's ability to control their thoughts and emotions.

See the Mind and Life Institute (www.mindandlife.org) for information about the benefits of meditation.

Outcomes

Students can demonstrate achievement at levels 4–6 in these activities if they can say 'yes' to some of these 'I can' statements:

Description of achievement:
I can . . .

Level 4

- describe how meditation might affect a Buddhist's day-to-day life
- express the impact of meditation through a poem or artwork, applying the ideas to myself.

Level 5

- use Buddhist words to explain Buddhist teachings on meditation and its importance in the lives of Buddhists
- explain my own views of spiritual practices, relating my ideas to Buddhist practices of meditation.

Level 6

- give an informed account of different ways in which Buddhists practise meditation
- express my insight into the value of meditation, for Buddhists and non-Buddhists, showing my understanding of at least two different viewpoints.

Activity 1
Experiencing stillness

Explain to the students:

- Buddhists are taught that it helps to meditate with others and learn from a teacher.
- As Buddhist meditation is a religious practice, it is not appropriate to do it in the RE classroom. However we can encounter some aspects of meditation by taking part in non-religious stilling exercises.

Take the students through the three stilling exercises on this page. Start off with a preparation for stilling exercise.

After each activity allow the students to record their ideas, thoughts and feelings about the stilling experience briefly on the recording sheet on p.13.

Explain the form of a haiku with the students, sharing the model from Basho. Ask students to use their notes from p.13 to help them to write a haiku reflecting their experience of stilling.

Some student examples are available online to subscribers 

Sample preparation for stilling script

Sit comfortably . . . with your back straight . . . feet on the floor . . . hands in your lap . . . relaxed . . .

let your eyes close gently . . . or look at the floor . . . so as not to distract others . . .

breathe slowly and silently . . . noticing the way your breath enters and leaves your body . . .

as you breathe in . . . begin counting (in your mind) . . . each time you breathe in, count to four . . . one . . . two . . . three . . . four . . .

each time you breathe out, count to four . . . one . . . two . . . three . . . four . . . and then start again . . .

as your mind wanders, bring it back gently and start from one again . . .

Sample script for recall stilling

Sit comfortably, with your back straight . . . focus on your breathing . . .

Take your mind back to the moment you woke up this morning . . .

Imagine the moment when you first begin to open your eyes, the moment when you became aware of the light through your eyelids . . . What was the first sound you heard?

Imagine the sensation of lying on the bed, under the duvet . . .

Slowly replay your day from this point onwards . . . try to recall everything that happened . . . make yourself aware of what you saw, felt, heard, smelt and tasted . . .

(Allow the students three or four minutes, or as long as they are able to engage with the activity to imagine their morning.)

Now, draw your attention back to your breathing . . . focus on the in-breath . . . the out-breath . . . Begin to be aware of the noises in the classroom around you . . . When you are ready, open your eyes . . .

(As the students open their eyes . . . ask them to use the resource sheet to record significant words to describe their recall stilling exercise. Then talk with them about how far they managed to replay their experiences. Some will have whizzed through the day, others will still be recalling the sensation of stepping out of bed . . .)

Sample script for mindfulness stilling

Sit comfortably, with your back straight . . . focus on your breathing . . .

Focus on your hands . . . be aware of how they feel . . . as they rest on your lap/table . . . can you sense the air touching them, the blood flowing through them . . . ?

Now turn your focus on your shoulders . . . be aware of the sensation of your shirt on your shoulders . . .

Direct your concentration on your feet . . . how do they feel? Be aware of your shoes on your feet . . . focus on the sensations . . .

Bring your focus back to your breathing . . . become aware of the noises around you . . . When ready, open your eyes.

Sample script for calming stilling

Sit comfortably, with your back straight . . . focus on your breathing . . .

As you breathe in, tense up the muscles in your body . . . As you breathe out, relax them . . .

(Repeat)

Recall something that you are worried about . . . As you think about it, feel the knot of tension and anxiety in your body . . .

Breathe out and relax, feel the knot untangle . . . Breathe out the tension . . . anxiety . . . worry . . .

Breathe in a feeling of peace . . .

Breathe in a feeling of relaxation . . .

Call to mind a person you want to bring happiness to . . . imagine that you are sharing peace with that person . . .

(Pause)

Now return your focus to your breathing . . . Be aware of noises around you . . . When you are ready, open your eyes . . .

Activity 2   Experiencing stillness

a Recall

b Mindfulness

c Calming

© Guido Vrola - Fotolia.com

Activity 3   Expressing insight

Haiku: a short poem, expressing insight.
Structure:
5 syllables
7 syllables
5 syllables
e.g.

Sick as a journey –
over sun-soaked rain-parched fields
my dreams wander on.

(after Basho)

You're going to write your own haiku to reflect your experiences of stilling today.
Think carefully. Use your notes from the stilling exercises (p.13).
Draft some ideas.
Take about 20 minutes.
Plan your words to fit the haiku structure.

Your finished poem should get across:
• something of how you **felt** during stilling and also
• what **impact** it might have on the person taking part in a stilling exercise or meditation.

My haiku

____

____

____

By _______________

Buddhist meditation: the information

Meditation involves getting rid of things that disturb the mind. These are sometimes called poisons or impurities. They include: desire, hatred, laziness, restlessness, worry.

Meditation involves developing skilful states, such as concentration, awareness, peace, loving-kindness, energy, confidence, tranquillity, joy.

Following the Eightfold Path helps someone to develop skilful states and gradually wear away the opposite 'wrong' factors, until all unskilful states are destroyed.

Samatha ('calm') meditation is used to develop concentration and calmness. It involves being able to develop single-pointed concentration, or discipline over a scattered mind. This form of meditation is now widely used by people who are not Buddhists.

Vipashyana (vipassana) ('insight') meditation is practised in order to understand the true nature of things. It is not about getting occasional flashes of insight. Vipashyana means 'seeing things as they really are'. This can lead to Enlightenment, the ultimate goal of Buddhist practice.

The Buddha talked about non-grasping. People often think non-grasping refers only to objects or people. But in truth, non-grasping means not clinging to our feelings and emotions. We need to let go of our inner feelings, but not to reject them, thinking: 'I don't want these feelings'. To let go, you don't really need to do anything: you just sit and be aware of what is happening in your mind.

Lama Yeshe Losal

I sit down to meditate for 30–60 minutes almost every day, very happily. The strange thing is I am very distracted, even after 18 years! Yet it still has an effect. I am more aware of my thoughts and emotions, moment by moment. That makes me more aware of what I am about to do and say, so I can make better choices. When I speak or behave in a hurtful way I am quicker to spot it and apologise.

Munisha

The point of meditation practice is the practice – whether or not it brings benefits, and sometimes it's hard. The mind does all sorts of things on its own – stirring up difficult memories, for example, that need to be observed and faced. Meditation does increase mindfulness in daily living, gradually, so that one becomes more aware of actions, words and thoughts and the impact they may have.

Joyce Miller

You should first . . . fill yourself with loving-kindness (metta).

Next you can recall kind words or actions that inspire love; then recall good behaviour in someone, that inspires respect.

Then develop loving-kindness towards that person by saying 'May this good person be happy and free from suffering.'

This helps you to reach full concentration (dhyana/jhana).

Buddhaghosa, in *Visuddhimagga*, 9.11

Activity 3   Exploring Buddhist meditation

Look carefully at the cards from p.15.

a   In pairs, see if you can make links between any of the cards. Place them so that cards that have strong links overlap; if there is a small link have the cards just touching. If there are no links, place the cards separately.

b   Take the outline below. Use it to **explain why Buddhists meditate**, from the information you have learned on the cards. For example, you might write down outside the outline the things that are taken away through meditation. You might write inside the outline the skilful habits that are developed.

c   Create your own artwork. The title is '**Meditation: in search of . . .**' Try to show something of what meditation means to Buddhists, using images, colours, symbols and words. You can use your own experiences of stilling, if you think that will help.

d   Write a short paragraph to explain your artwork, and to answer the questions: Why do Buddhists meditate? What can I learn from this?

RE Today
Services

WHAT WISDOM DOES THE DHARMA HAVE FOR BUDDHISTS AND FOR ME?

Summary of learning

Buddhist Dharma (P. Dhamma) is one of the 'Three Jewels' of Buddhism – Buddhists begin religious acts by going for refuge to the Enlightened One (the Buddha), the Teaching (Dharma) and the Community (Sangha).

Aimed at **students aged 11–14**, this unit explores ways in which the Buddha's teachings (Dharma/Dhamma) express key Buddhist understandings of the world. The Buddha offers a path for his followers that combines wisdom, morality and the practice of mindfulness.

A wide range of Buddhist texts explore the teachings of the Buddha, and one significant feature is the use of vivid imagery to put the message across. The resources on these pages do not seek to give a systematic account of Buddhist teachings. Instead, they select some vivid similes and metaphors as ways into some important teachings. These are used to illuminate a Buddhist way of viewing the world and deepen students' understanding of Buddhism, as well as enabling them to consider their own worldview.

The pages also include accounts of the importance of different texts and teachings in the lives of representatives of four Buddhist traditions. This rich, contemporary, flexible, insider resource offers a window into the similarities and differences between Buddhist traditions.

Extended versions of the interviews on pp. 22-23 are available to RE Today subscribers: www.retoday.org.uk

Using the pages

Copy pp.18–21 for students. Get them to work through the activities on each page. Cutting up the boxes on pp.18 and 19 will allow them to do the sorting and matching exercises easily.

For the teacher

The term Dharma has many resonances. It is used to refer to the teaching of the Buddha (Buddhadharma) as well as a specific view of reality. The Buddhadharma includes the Four Noble Truths, ideas of impermanence (anitya/anicca) and no-self (anatman/anatta), two of the three marks of existence (the third, duhkha, is explored on pp. 5–11) and doctrines of karma (kamma) and nirvana (nibbana).

As explored on pp.5–11, the Buddha diagnoses the problem of duhkha and offers a cure and a prescription. The term *duhkha (dukkha)* has been translated as suffering, stress and unsatisfactoriness in the different translations used on p.19.

Note that the dedication from Shantideva mentioned on p.23 can be found on p.4. It is from the *Bodhicaryavatara*. The prayer used in the section on Aung San Suu Kyi (p.26) is also from this text.

Resources

www.accesstoinsight.org

Many texts from the Pali Theravada tradition can be found here in a clear translation, together with helpful articles explaining Buddhist texts and teachings. This site includes a fascinating index of similes:

http://www.accesstoinsight.org/index-similes.html

Outcomes

Students can demonstrate achievement at levels 4–6 in these activities if they can say 'yes' to some of these 'I can' statements:

Description of achievement:
I can . . .

Level 4

- make links between some images in Buddhist texts and some key Buddhist teachings
- refer to Buddhist teachings when giving my own response to suffering and change in life.

Level 5

- explain how following the teachings of the Buddha makes a difference in the lives of two Buddhists
- express my own views about the Buddhist understanding that all of life is unsatisfactory.

Level 6

- interpret Buddhist texts and interviews with Buddhists in order to explain how and why traditions and practices vary
- consider the challenges and possible benefits of following the Buddha's teachings in a culture like the UK, where many people like to have lots of stuff
- express insights into the value of meditation, showing my understanding of a religious perspective and an awareness of different views.

What lessons could we learn from the world around us?

In small groups, look at the following images. What do you think we might learn from them for our everyday lives? For example, the building site may make us think that we should study hard so that we have good foundations for later life. There are many possible lessons to be learned, so be creative!

© Copyright Walter Baxter and licensed for reuse under this Creative Commons Licence.

© Scott Cramer

© Alan Crawford

© Kimpin - Fotolia.com

© Rick Olson

RE Today Services

What do Buddhists learn from the world around them?

Cut out the boxes. Match the text to the image from p.18. See if you can sort these into groups – are there any links between the texts? There is no single correct answer to this, so look for any links you can see.

Just as a dewdrop on the tip of a blade of grass quickly vanishes with the rising of the sun and does not stay long, in the same way . . . the life of human beings is like a dewdrop – limited, trifling, of much stress and many despairs. *Anguttara Nikaya*, 7.70 (Access to Insight)	No one can claim to bring an end to suffering without understanding the first three Noble Truths. It would be the same as if someone said, 'I am going to build the first floor of a house before I build the ground floor.' That would be impossible. Adapted from *Samyutta Nikaya*, 56:44	What you do with body, speech, or mind: that is yours; that's your follower, like a shadow that never leaves. Thus you should do what is good as a stash for the next life. Acts of merit are the support for beings in their after-death world. *Samyutta Nikaya*, 3:20 (Access to Insight)
As the blade of a plough slices through any roots in the ground, so if you properly understand impermanence – that will remove all desire and delusion of 'I am'. Adapted from *Amyutta Nikaya*, 22:102	Just as one would put out a burning refuge with water, so does the enlightened one blow away any arisen grief and sorrow, like the wind blows away a bit of cotton fluff. *Sutta Nipatta*, 3:8 (Access to Insight)	Just as a line drawn in the water with a stick quickly vanishes and does not stay long, in the same way . . . the life of human beings is like a line drawn in the water with a stick – limited, trifling, of much stress and many despairs. *Anguttara Nikaya*, 7.70 (Access to Insight)
Like a deep lake, clear, unruffled, and calm: so the wise become clear, calm, on hearing words of the Dhamma. *Dhammapada* 82 (Access to Insight)	'Greed, I say, is a great flood; it is a whirlpool sucking you down, a constant yearning, seeking a hold, continually in movement; difficult to cross is the swamp of sensual desire.' *Attadanda Sutta* (Access to Insight)	All that we are is the result of our mind; it is founded on the results of our actions and experiences; our life is the creation of our mind. If a person speaks or acts with an impure mind, pain follows that person, as the wheel follows the foot of the ox that draws the carriage. Adapted from *Dhammapada 1*
Imagine a huge fire, made of 40 cartloads of timber. A man keeps throwing more stuff onto it – and, being fed like this, the fire burns for a long, long time. This is just like a person who keeps focusing on the attraction of clingable stuff. In that person, craving arises. Adapted from *Uppadana Sutta*	I see living beings . . . lacking wisdom, entering the path of birth and death. They are firmly tied to desires like a yak is to its tail. They smother themselves with greed and love, blind, and in darkness, seeing nothing. They do not seek the mighty Buddha, or the Dharma which cuts off suffering. But instead . . . with suffering, they wish to cast off suffering. *Lotus Sutra 2*	How is the body cleaned? Through the use of scrubbing brushes and soap and the appropriate human effort. In the same way, the defiled mind is cleansed through the proper technique. When the disciple recalls the Dhamma, his mind is cleansed, and joy arises; the defilements of his mind are abandoned. Adapted from *Anguttara Nikaya*, 3: 70

In pairs, choose at least four of the questions that you would like to answer from the grid below. Match them up with an image from p.18 and a teaching from p.19. Then have a go at coming up with some thoughtful answers.

1 Imagine the sun drying up the ground after a rain shower. In what ways could you say that life is like this?	**2** Give an example of when you have tried to 'run before you can walk' – tried to do something difficult without getting the basics right. What happened?	**3** What difference would it make if you knew that everything you did – good or bad – would come back on you? If you could be sure that all your deeds will have consequences?
4 Is anything easy? If someone told you 'Five easy steps to exam success' or 'The easy path to happiness', would you believe them? Why/why not?	**5** Give two reasons why greed might lead to unhappiness. What do you think about greed?	**6** In what ways may grief and sorrow be like a fire? Can you think of ways of overcoming these painful emotions?
7 Can you say what it is like when your mind is in turmoil? How did it feel? Is there anything that brings calm to a fizzing mind?	**8** If the universe is billions of years old, consider how living for 80–90 years is just a blink in comparison. How does that make you think and feel?	**9** How far do you agree that you are the result of your previous actions and experiences? Are there parts of your life that are not created by your mind?
10 Are you moved when you see suffering? What do you think is the cause of suffering?	**11** Think about when you really wanted to own something. How do you feel when you eventually get it? For how long does it satisfy? What happens next?	**12** Think of as many things as you can that never change.

RE Today
Services

Buddhist teachings

1 In pairs, match the images and texts from pp.18 and 19 to the teachings below.

2 When you have matched them, write a short explanation of your own, using the ideas from the texts. How do these help to explain the teachings?

3 When you have done this, come up with at least one more image or simile of your own to explain the teaching.

Anitya/Anicca (impermanence)

The Buddha taught that nothing is permanent. Everything changes. The world is made up of lots of different elements called dharmas. Human beings consist of 'bundles' of these dharmas. As we are made of these changing bundles of dharmas, we are not permanent or lasting either. We may experience moments of happiness and joy, and moments of pain and misery, but these will change. Life is fleeting and we should not cling to it.

Trishna/Tanha (craving/thirst)

The Buddha taught that the reason why human life is full of unsatisfactoriness (duhkha/dukkha) is because we crave stuff. We want to hang on to things and experiences for ourselves, and to avoid unpleasant experiences. However, this leads to frustration – things never last, and even if we have pleasant experiences, we always want more! These cravings can lead to conflict with others.

Karma/Kamma (actions)

The Buddha taught that all beings are reborn according to their past deeds. As human beings, then, we are inheritors of our past actions. The quality of our actions moulds the kind of person we will be in a subsequent life. Like a seed, our actions ripen into fruit in this life or another. All desires, intentions and actions matter because they have consequences and effects. We should try and be skilful in our actions, developing a healthy state of mind.

Dharma/Dhamma (teaching)

Buddhists believe that the Buddha discovered the truth about the nature of life and living. The truths he discovered are called the Dharma – these are the natural laws of the universe. The Buddha's teaching of these truths is also called the Dharma. Buddhism itself is all about understanding and practising the Dharma. Doing this can lead to freedom from suffering and unsatisfactoriness.

Voices from Buddhism: what the Dharma means to me

Rev. Alicia Rowe
Order of Buddhist Contemplatives
Throssel Hole Buddhist Abbey

Srivati
Bodhi Tree
London Buddhist Centre

To which Buddhist tradition do you belong?

I belong to the Soto Zen tradition, which originated in Japan. The founder of our Order, an Englishwoman named Rev. Master Jiyu-Kennett, trained as a monk at Sojiji, one of the head temples of our tradition in Japan.

To which Buddhist tradition do you belong?

I belong to the Triratna Buddhist Order which used to be known as the Western Buddhist Order. 'Triratna' means 'Three Jewels' which is another way of saying the three most precious things in Buddhism, true for all of us: the Buddha, the Dharma and the Sangha.

What are the most important texts in your tradition?

Our tradition was founded by Great Master Eihei Dogen (1200–1253 CE) so his works, especially the *Shobogenzo* are very important. Also *The Lotus Sutra*, which profoundly influenced Dogen.

What are the most important texts in your tradition?

We don't have any one particular text, as we have access to so many in translation here in the West, from the Dhammapada to *The Life and Liberation of Padmasambhava*, which comes from Tibet.

What stories and teachings have an impact on your daily life? How?

I guess the teaching of the Four Noble Truths, that suffering is caused by attachment and that there is a way to live your life that lets go of attachment and finds peace and complete satisfaction by living in harmony with the universe. When we stop running away from pain and dissatisfaction, especially when we stop attaching to the thoughts in our own minds and no longer take them as truth, we actually find that there is nothing to be afraid of, that a life lived with integrity and authenticity gives one the greatest peace of mind.

What stories and teachings have an impact on your daily life? How?

There are so many of them! The teachings on mindfulness are invaluable, because trying to become more aware covers everything, whether it's how I talk to people, what and how I eat or remembering that nothing stays the same so why get so worried about stuff … Also the teachings on compassion. The Buddha met so many different kinds of people and in each case what he said was appropriate to them, whether a king, a killer like Angulimala or a bereaved mother like Kisa Gotami. Both of their stories remind me that we can change for the better and see things more clearly.

What is your favourite story or saying? Why?

In the *Majjhima Nikaya*, the Buddha visits three monks living in the Eastern Bamboo Park. He says: 'I hope, Anuruddha, that you are all living in concord, with mutual appreciation, without disputing, blending like milk and water, viewing each other with kindly eyes.' Anuruddha replies that they are and he goes on to give examples of how they live together 'blending like milk and water'.

This story really struck me as an example of how people could live together in harmony.

What is your favourite story or saying? Why?

'If in doubt, give.' This helps others (if I have no money, I can always give my time or even just be friendly with a smile) and helps me to be less self-obsessed or selfish. And if I'm feeling bad, it makes *me* feel better too.

Do you have a wise piece of advice for teenagers from a text or teacher?

The Buddha advised people not to accept his teaching just because it was him saying it, but to find out for themselves if it was really true. In other words, think for yourself, find out for yourself what is true, what brings about joy and peace for yourself and others. Do not blindly follow anyone or any teaching. Do not be afraid of what other people will think of you. Cultivate your awareness and compassion and follow your own heart.

Do you have a wise piece of advice for teenagers from a text or teacher?

If you're confused, angry, upset or over-excited, just stop and breathe in, and notice that you're breathing in; then breathe out, and notice what that feels like. This is the shortest meditation in the world and can often help you let go and move on or make a wiser decision about what happens next.

RE Today Services

Voices from Buddhism: what the Dharma means to me

Dr Joyce Miller	Venerable Tenzin Choesang
To which Buddhist tradition do you belong? The Thai Forest Sangha. It is a very simple and pure form of Theravada Buddhism, and the monks and nuns of the tradition have to live a very strict life. The practice of mindfulness is key in this tradition, which leads to a quietness and simplicity in the life and practice of the communities.	**To which Buddhist tradition do you belong?** To the Tibetan Tradition. There are four main lineages, often referred to as 'schools', of Tibetan tradition: Gelugpa, Nygma, Sakya and Kagyu. I personally belong to the Gelugpa lineage. This is the one that His Holiness the 14th Dalai Lama comes from. His Holiness is the head of all Tibetan Buddhist lineages.
What are the most important texts in your tradition? Texts play a relatively unimportant part in the life of this tradition. We use the published teachings of some of our senior monks, such as Ajahn Chah and Ajahn Sumedho.	**What are the most important texts in your tradition?** The *Sūtras* of Shakyamuni Buddha. *Lam Rim* and *Mahamudra*, which are the guidelines for Buddhists to learn the philosophy of Buddhism. The *Tengyur* and *Kangyur*, which are the complete translations of the Buddha's *Sūtras*, and guidelines for living as a monastic within Buddhism.
What stories and teachings have an impact on your daily life? How? The practice of meditation is most important in my tradition, rather than the stories and teachings in the scriptures. The Buddha presents a coherent, unified teaching. The Eightfold Path, for example, is a whole, not to be followed sequentially. Practising one step will have an impact on the others. For example, if you follow the Buddha's teaching on morality (sila) then you have to be mindful – not harming a living being, not saying anything that is hurtful or false. Being mindful means deeper awareness and concentration; that improves one's meditation practice and therefore aids the development of wisdom. It's the Buddha's wisdom that I admire – and I see it in the teachings, lives and example of the monks and nuns.	**What stories and teachings have an impact on your daily life? How?** **The Tong Len practice**, which is a practice of taking the pain from other people and using this to diminish one's negative karmic residue. **The Six Yogas of Naropa**. These are yogic practices to enable one to reach full Buddhahood in the fastest possible time. **The Tibetan Book of the Dead**. This is a profound teaching of the various stages of dying and one's rebirth. When one is starting out on one's Buddhist path, the ***Lam Rim***, or the ***Stages of Mahamudra*** gives the foundation teachings of the philosophy of Buddhism.
What is your favourite story or saying? Why? Almost any verse from the **Dhammapada**. I try to remember to read sayings from it every day because I need constant reminders about the path I am trying to follow. It's not easy and the support of the Sangha (community) is vital for my practice. My other favourite is the Buddha's words on loving-kindness which include: *Even as a mother protects with her life* *Her child, her only child,* *So with a boundless heart* *Should one cherish all living beings . . .*	**What is your favourite story or saying? Why?** The Life Story of the Buddha. The version ***Old Path White Clouds*** by Thich Nhat Hanh is a lovely read about the Buddha's life and connects me to the roots of my reason for being a practising Buddhist. The prayer of dedication from ***A Guide to the Bodhissatva's Way of Life*** by Shantideva, a Buddhist master from India in the eighth century CE, is also a favourite. It is one of His Holiness the Dalai Lama's favourite prayers, and is important to many Buddhists, particularly those from the Tibetan traditions. (See p.4 for this prayer.)
Do you have a wise piece of advice for teenagers from a text or teacher? Be mindful!	**Do you have a wise piece of advice for teenagers from a text or teacher?** Learn how to meditate. It does not have to be as a part of any Buddhist religion. It helps you to control and then diminish negative attitudes such as anger; to prepare yourself for exams by developing and de-cluttering the brain; and it helps you to feel calm, to make wiser decisions and to sleep well.

Learning from Buddhists in Britain today

1 Read the information on pp.22–3. In pairs, take the comments from one of the Buddhists. See if their words can help you to add anything to the information you have filled in about Buddhist teachings on p.21.

2 Using the evidence in the interviews, what do you imagine each Buddhist would say to complete the sentence starters below? The answers are not given directly – you will need to look for clues and then, using what you already know about Buddhism, come up with your best ideas. Fill this grid in for one interview, then take it in turns to share with other pairs who have been looking at different interviews.

Rev. Alicia Rowe / Srivati / Dr Joyce Miller / Venerable Tenzin Choesang might say . . .

Every day I . . .	For myself, I would like . . .
For other people in the world, I would like . . .	**Buddhism's gift to the world would be . . .**

3 From this information, decide in your group:
   - what things are important to **all four** of the Buddhist traditions represented here
   - what things matter **to two** of the traditions
   - what things are **distinctive** to each tradition (i.e. is there anything that has only been mentioned by one of the Buddhists here?)

4 Having explored some Buddhist teachings and heard from some Buddhists, what questions would you like to ask? In your group, come up with at least five questions.

5 The Buddha offers a way of understanding life. Are there **three insights** that you have found helpful as you explore these teachings? What have you learned from them?

Summary of learning

This unit uses a real-life story to provoke challenging questions about the decisions we make and the service of others. It connects Buddhist scripture and meditation to social and political action in the contemporary world, an example of 'engaged Buddhism'.

The activities make a suitable assessment for a unit of work on Buddhism in the **12–14 age group**, but could also be used to assess work on inspiring leaders, on the global contexts of religion, or on the impact of faith on daily life. It can also make a strong contribution to students' spiritual and moral development.

The story is about the great contemporary Buddhist, Aung San Suu Kyi, leader of Burma's National League for Democracy and winner of the Nobel Peace Prize in 1991. Thinking skills activities enable students to weigh up evidence and make thoughtful judgements. The focus of the work is on making difficult decisions – good teaching will enable students to think about their own big decisions in the light of their learning about Aung San Suu Kyi.

The story told is a tough one, but RE does not shy away from difficult themes and questions: this story is powerful because it deals with 'love and death'. Of course, sensitive handling in the light of the students' experiences will be important.

A PowerPoint to support this work is available to subscribers on the RE Today website. It includes examples of students' work and more learning tasks.

Resources

- **The Lady:** released on DVD in April 2012, this full-length feature film tells the story used here. We recommend you select some short clips. Offer a chance to see the whole film as an after-school extra to pupils.
- Liam Gearon, *A Noble Life: The Story of Aung San Suu Kyi,* (RMEP 2004).
- Burma Solidarity: www burmacampaign.org.uk
- Deborah Helme, *A Powerful Voice: The Story of Bono of U2* (RMEP 2004).
- The U2 song: 'Walk On', is dedicated to Aung San Suu Kyi, from the CD *All That You Can't Leave Behind.* Play it to your students and get them to explain the lyrics.
- There is useful guidance using this example on RE APP (Assessing Pupil Progress) on the NATRE website: www.natre.org.uk

Outcomes

Students can demonstrate achievement at levels 4–7 in these activities if they can say 'yes' to some of these 'I can' statements:

Description of achievement:
I can . . .

Level 4

- show that I understand what difference being a Buddhist made to Aung San Suu Kyi
- apply the teaching of the Buddha to Aung San's decision for myself, thoughtfully
- apply a Buddhist idea to my own life, simply (using a '**what would you do if . . .?** formula)
- use some Buddhist terminology to show my understanding.

Level 5

- explain clearly some connections between Buddhist ideas and Aung San's life, using Buddhist terminology correctly
- ask, and suggest answers to questions of commitment and value from the case study, and from my own life
- express my own views of the actions and consequences on Aung San's dilemma, referring to religious teaching.

Level 6

- use a religious and philosophical vocabulary to give an informed and coherent account of the impact of the Buddha's teaching on Aung San Suu Kyi
- interpret the dilemma she faced with reference to religious, political and social sources of information
- express my own insights into issues of duty, compassion and family loyalty arising from the case study.

Level 7

- account for the influences on Aung San's dilemma using philosophical and religious ideas and placing the dilemma in a social and political context
- use a philosophical and religious vocabulary to analyse the impact of Buddhist teaching
- articulate personal and critical responses to this and another issue of human rights and justice.

Activity 1   Big decisions

Give each student two strips of paper – these can be used later for a display on 'big decisions'. What is the biggest decision they have made this month? On one strip, pupils write the big decision. On the second strip they write what happened because of that decision.

Get pupils to roll the strip of paper tightly round a pencil, so that it stays curled. They can be pinned/stapled to the display, in such a way that if you want to read them you can uncurl them one by one. The idea of the display is that we can get 'twisted up' about big decisions, but thinking about what will happen next can help us.

Activity 2   Slow walking

One kind of Buddhist meditation practice is to walk as slowly and mindfully as possible, taking careful note and paying attention to all aspects of the movement of walking. Try this as a 'way to stillness' and mindfulness for students.

If the day is fine, walking along a line in the playground, or across the field (can this be done harmlessly?), while noting the movement, muscles, breathing, sight and sounds of the walk is an interesting activity.

Nelson Mandela said 'There is no easy walk to Freedom anywhere'. Later, you can discuss with the students what Aung San Suu Kyi might say about her own walk in life, and about 'walking as a Buddhist'. Encourage students to think of their own lives as 'a walk through the world'. What kind of walk is theirs?

Activity 3
Aung San Suu Kyi's story

Use p.27. Don't tell the class how the story ends: the dilemma learning activity depends on them not knowing what happened. It is best for the teacher to retell this story dramatically, but an alternative is to give students the page to read for themselves.

The students might collect answers to these questions as they listen:

* Who is Aung Sang Suu Kyi?
* Where does she live?
* What is the situation in her country?
* Why does she meditate?
* What is her dilemma?

Meditation on the image of the Buddha is an important spiritual practice for many Buddhists: they seek a mindful, calm, determined approach to life that reduces suffering and pursues Enlightenment.

Activity 4
Thinking about Buddhist meditation

Read the text from the Bodhicaryavatara (see below). This text is used by many Buddhists to help them see how to live compassionately.

Ask students:

Do they want to be any of these things: a protector, a guide, like a boat, bridge or raft; like a lamp, a home to the homeless, a servant to the world? In what ways, for whom and why?

Teach them that the Bodhicaryavatara was written about 1300 years ago by a Buddhist monk called Shantideva, and is a text many Buddhists have used for 13 centuries to inspire, discipline and guide their lives.

May I be a protector of the helpless;
a guide to those travelling the path;
a boat to those wishing to cross over,
or a bridge, or a raft.
May I be a lamp for those in darkness,
a home for the homeless,
a servant to the world.

Bodhicaryavatara, chapter 3:16–8

Aung San Suu Kyi's dilemma: stay or go?

Aung San Suu Kyi was born in 1945. Her father was a great leader in her country, Burma, and people called him 'the father of the nation'. She was clever, determined and well educated, so she won a place at the University of Oxford, where she met and fell in love with her future husband Michael. They had two sons Alexander and Kim, who were born in 1972 and 1977.

In 1962 the army generals took control of Burma and brutally repressed all opposition. For many years, there was no relief for the poor, the minorities and increasingly for any of the Burmese people. The generals did not want the people to choose their own leader and would not allow democracy. The government delivered hunger, imprisonment and violence.

In 1988, Aung San Suu Kyi's mother had a stroke. Like any good Buddhist, Aung San Suu Kyi went to Rangoon, the capital city, to nurse her mother, leaving her boys, now 11 and 17, in Oxford with Michael, their father. She was appalled at the violence and repression of the government. There was a big campaign to change Burma through a vote for a new government. Because people remembered her father so well and loved what the country had been like in his day, many leaders persuaded Aung San to lead the National League for Democracy.

As well as caring for her mother, she became a candidate for election, touring the country, speaking to huge crowds. Once at the Shwedagon Temple in 1989, half a million people turned up to hear her. When the votes were counted in 1990 Aung San Suu Kyi had won more than 8 out of 10 – over 80 per cent of the votes.

Immediately the army changed their minds. Soldiers came, arrested Aung San Suu Kyi, and kept her locked up in her own home (under house arrest). The army never let her take over as leader. They carried on with their old ways. Aung San won the famous Nobel Peace Prize in 1991, but was not allowed to go and collect it. Her son went to Norway to read a speech she had written, and collected it on her behalf.

The generals in Burma refused Michael, Alexander and Kim permission to visit Aung San. They forced Aung San Suu Kyi to stay locked up in her own house, even though she had committed no crime. They were scared of the fact that the Burmese people loved her, and they thought if she wasn't under arrest, then their rule over the country would be threatened. She had three brief visits from Michael, Alexander and Kim over the next six years. Then all visits were stopped.

Alone, she learned the Buddhist scriptures, listened to the BBC on her radio, and refused to leave the country. The generals would have loved to see the back of her! Four more years passed like this.

In 1999, after ten years under arrest, working to help the people of Burma from her house in Rangoon, Aung San Suu Kyi was missing her husband terribly. One morning she got a letter from Michael: dreadful news from Oxford. Michael was ill – seriously ill. He had cancer, and he was dying. The doctors said he would die in twelve weeks.

Aung San's first wish was to rush to Oxford and be with him, but then she realised that the generals wouldn't ever let her back into the country of Burma if she left. She would become an exile. She would never lead her people to freedom. The hopes of the Burmese would be dashed.

A terrible decision had to be made. If she went to Oxford, she would never be allowed to return to Burma and help her people there. Her freedom struggle would be over. If she stayed in Rangoon, she would never see her husband again. She would not even be able to go to his funeral. She would not be able to comfort her sons in their mourning, or receive their comfort.

> Imagine that Aung San asks you for advice. What would you say? What should she do?
> In pairs, come up with two pieces of advice.

Activity 5
Debating the dilemma

Page 29 gives the advice that Aung San Suu Kyi received about her terrible decision. Copy the page onto card and cut up enough sets for students to work in groups of three.

Ask each student to study three of the pieces of advice. Then students must put the nine pieces in order from 'most useful advice' to 'least helpful advice'. Then they should discuss the decision, and write down what they think Aung San Suu Kyi should do, in the light of all the advice. They should give at least three reasons for their advice.

You might play the U2 song 'Walk On' while small groups discuss the pieces of advice and agree their own points of view.

Take a vote (no abstentions!): should she stay in Rangoon or go to Oxford?

Activity 6
Considering Buddhist teaching

The next stage of the activity will be to consider how Aung San's decision reflected Buddhist teachings. First of all the students need to know what she did decide.

The decision: Aung San Suu Kyi took a week to make her mind up, and decided to stay in Burma. It was the only way she could be a 'servant to the world'. Her husband Michael died without seeing his wife again after twelve weeks. Ten years later she was finally released. In April 2012, she won another election in Burma, taking 97 per cent of the seats contested for the National League for Democracy.

Display the text from Shantideva (below) on the whiteboard. Ask students:

- Describe how these lines have come true, or been put into practice in Aung San Suu Kyi's life.
- Would any of them wish to be like the person Shantideva (the author) describes? Why? Why not?
- A line-by-line analysis of this deepens the learning and connects it to Buddhist tradition. You might also connect her way of life to the Noble Eightfold Path.

Clearly this stage of the activity will vary according to how much your students know about Buddhism. If this assessment activity is used at the end of a unit of work on Buddhism, then the teachings and sources the students have encountered will inform their work, enabling achievement at higher levels.

Activity 7
Dilemma no 2: facing death

Use the information on p.30 to outline a second dilemma Aung San faced. Retell the story, pausing at the point of decision. Ask students to decide what the options are, what Aung San could do and what they think she might do. Ask students to refer to Buddhist teachings in their discussions.

For example, in the Buddha's teachings, the fact of death and the acceptance of impermanence are key ideas. How might this affect Aung San's actions?

Complete the story.

Reflect on the Buddhist quotation and ask students to think of people who might also stand out as examples of goodness in some dark and difficult places in the world.

Activity 8
Getting creative

Ask students to imagine that the city of Oxford has decided to honour Aung San Suu Kyi with a monument. In groups of three, students must:

a design the most appropriate monument

b write a short statement to go on a bronze plaque beside the monument that explains its significance

c write a short speech for the Mayor of Oxford to give at the monument's unveiling.

They must choose images and words to express the story of Aung San Suu Kyi in ways that will inspire others to care about Burma, and which reveal their understanding of how her Buddhist beliefs have shaped her responses to life.

The results of this activity can be used alongside the display of personal decisions from Activity 1.

May I be a protector of the helpless;
a guide to those travelling the path;
a boat to those wishing to cross over,
or a bridge, or a raft.
May I be a lamp for those in darkness,
a home for the homeless,
a servant to the world.

Bodhicaryavatara, chapter 3:16–8

A friend's advice: 'The Generals have been in charge of Burma since 1962. They use their large army to prevent anyone who disagrees with them from speaking up. They threaten and imprison people who speak against them. Why stay, Aung San? You can leave. Go to be with Michael in Oxford. He is your husband and he needs you. *Don't feel bad about not being able to come back.*

Michael's advice: 'Dear Aung San – we have been married 27 years. We've been through many difficulties. I miss you terribly at this sad time, facing death from cancer. The doctors are quite clear: they will not be able to save me. I would love to see you, and be with you after our four years apart. But *you must do what you think is right.*'

One of Aung San's advisers reminds her of something she said to her people: 'Change will come. The Generals will not win. All they have is the guns. They will lose.' She asks: *'If you leave now, and do not return, do you think the Generals will be stronger or weaker because you're not here?'*

Another friend's advice is this: 'The Burmese people chose you to be their leader. In 1990, 80 per cent of the people of Burma voted for you, Aung San. We know the army Generals who rule Burma won't allow you to rule the nation yet. But as long as you are here, the people have hope. Please don't leave us just because you can. The Generals want you to leave and never come back. *Why should you do what they want?'*

The advice of the Generals who rule in Burma is very clear. They offer Aung San Suu Kyi a choice: 'We think you're a troublemaker. You can leave Burma if you wish to see your husband before he dies. We will not let you return afterwards. Or you can stay. He will die. You will never see him again. *Go now, while you have the chance, and leave Burma in our hands.'*

Her son reminds Aung San of the speech he made for her at the Nobel Peace Prize giving in 1991. Her courage and determination in working for peace in Burma were praised. Her son accepted the prize for her because she was imprisoned. He said 'If she were here today, my mother would ask you to pray for the oppressors in Burma.' He advises: 'You must decide what is best for Burma, and best for you. *Meditate, and see what seems best.'*

Burma Solidarity Campaign is a charity for the friends of Burma who live in the UK. They ask Aung San to keep up the pressure for peace in Burma. They don't tell her what to do, but they do say *'You alone can focus the hopes of the world for a better future in your country.'*

U2's advice: from the song 'Walk On.'
Love is not the easy thing
If the darkness is to keep us apart,
If the daylight feels it's a long way off,
If your glass heart should crack,
Be strong, walk on.
What you've got, they can't steal it.
Walk on. Stay safe.

The Buddha taught: *'A person with compassion is kind, even when angry. For one with compassion, even enemies may turn into friends.'*
Aung San is a Buddhist.

Aung San's second dilemma: facing death

In April 1989, after her mother's death, Aung San was touring Burma to speak to the people about getting rid of the Generals' military junta and bringing freedom to the country. At various places on her tour, huge crowds gathered, but she travelled between the meetings in a small group: just a few of her supporters in a couple of cars.

Her supporters were often worried about this, because the military were rumoured to have called for her death, and soldiers were often seen. But Aung San told her supporters that the Buddhist virtues of fearlessness (abhaya) and non-violence (ahimsa) must guide them. 'It is the military who are full of fear,' she told them. 'That's why they are violent. Our way will be different.' Her followers were impressed, but sometimes still anxious.

On the road to a village where Aung San was to speak, their cars were stopped by a shouting group of soldiers, fully armed with automatic rifles. It was one of the Generals' death squads, intent on killing them all.

What should she do?

(Pause here, give pairs of students two minutes' discussion, and take ideas, and a vote on how she should behave.)

Quickly, Aung San stepped from the vehicle. She sent her supporters to the side of the road. 'It's better for them to have a single target,' she whispered. 'I don't want to bring you all into this.' She stepped lightly towards the soldiers.

The slight figure of a woman in her forties with a flower in her hair stood calmly in front of the armed gang, waiting for the bullets. Suddenly, strangely, they hesitated. No one fired. They looked mostly at the ground, then up from the corner of an eye. They saw a slender, fearless woman, unarmed, standing calmly before them – how could they shoot?

From the back of the squad, the commander, a major, pushed through. He gave new order: 'Stand down.' The death squad, relieved, stepped back, and pulled out of their road block. Aung San and her supporters got back into their cars, and drove on to speak of freedom, fearlessness and non-violence to their followers in the next village. The supporters were amazed. How did she do it? Where did she find the courage?

Buddhist scripture says 'A true follower of the Buddha shines among blind mortals like the sweet smelling lotus flower, growing in the garbage by the roadside, bringing joy to all who pass by.' (Dhammapada, 4:58-59).

In what ways does this scripture connect with the incident above?

ACCESS

Three ways to make some of the work in this book more accessible for lower-achieving students.

Use a Buddha image: select and write six words

This activity gives students an outline of a Buddha image, like the one below. After their study of the Buddha and Buddhism, they are invited to select six words from the twelve given below – all of these are mentioned by Joyce Miller (pp.2-3). They are 'things that matter' to Buddhists. Students should choose the six they think they can explain. Ask the students to write their six chosen words round the outside of the Buddha image. This can be done using tracing paper, so that a new image of the Buddha is created from the letters of the six words.

What is Buddhism all about? Choose from these words:

SPIRITUAL / MORAL / HAPPINESS / COMPASSION / BALANCE / BUDDHA / KINDNESS / THE PATH / NON-ATTACHMENT / MEDITATION / INSPIRATION / TEACHINGS

When they have done this, explain that for many Buddhists, the words and concepts of the tradition are all seen in the Buddha himself.

What do you wish for?

The activity that starts on p.5 asks students about what they wish for. This is already an accessible piece of work, but to further enable lower-achievers to get into the thinking give them this alternative.

Two pupils are doing their RE homework. The teacher has asked them to list five wishes each, then to split them into selfish wishes and compassionate wishes. Look at their answers, and talk to your partner before highlighting all the selfish ones in yellow and the compassionate ones in blue.

"We wished for...
A lottery win
Mum to be fit and well
My sister to leave me alone
A job with good pay
Top score on X-BOX
Double pocket money
Sunshine on Gran's birthday
Peace in the world
My cat to have kittens
No more RE homework"

The answers after discussion will show how well the students understand the key Buddhist idea of compassion. Are there some that lie between selfish and compassionate?
Here's an acrostic to discuss with them about it:

Caring for all life
Opening my life to others
Making time for those who suffer
Peacemaking in conflict
Asking how I can help
Sending love to all who need it
Spending my time for others
Including those others leave out
Opening my heart in kindness
Never giving up!

Stillness: What helps?

The section on pp.12-14 of the book asks students to think about the value of stillness. But it is not always easy to make stillness happen. Ask students to work with a partner to say what the ideal conditions for stilling might be. They can choose four things from this 'menu'.

It is easier to be still if. . .

. . . it is dark
. . . I am looking at a nice view
. . . I am lying down
. . . I am sitting
. . . I am alone
. . . I am in a small group
. . . I am listening to quiet music
. . . I am hearing running water
. . . there is no sound
. . . I have nothing to do
. . . I am stroking my pet
. . . there is sunshine

- Ask the pairs of students to listen to each others' 'recipe for stillness'. Are they the same or different?
- Ask them to report back what they chose to the class (it is good to put lower-achieving students in the 'driving seat' for learning sometimes).
- Ask them to notice that there are different ways to be still.
- Ask them if life without stillness is good. What makes stillness important?

This can lead on to work about how Buddhists use stillness for meditation: anyone can learn from this practice.

CHALLENGE

Three ways to make the work in this book more demanding of higher-achieving students.

The Four Sights: judging different retellings

Page 6 gives you several ideas about teaching the 'Four Sights'. Good tasks for more able students often require them to justify a judgement, so get your high-flying group to look at three or four different presentations of the four sights and rank them: which ones communicate the ideas of the story better, and which are less good?

A comic book, video clip, poem or written account and a drama might be viewed for this task.

Can your high-achievers offer any psychological explanations of why, after all his years in the pleasure palace of his father, the four sights affected Siddhartha Gautama so profoundly?

Is it ever a good idea to close your eyes to human experience, to shut someone away from reality?

Does our society shield children from death and pain? Too much, or about enough?

Our Eightfold Path / the Buddha's Eightfold Path

Gifted students often need to think fast and respond well to time deadlines. In this approach, their learning is accelerated. Note that asking for 'more detail' does not usually appeal, or indicate high achievement.

The work on p.6ff describes the Noble Eightfold Path, and develops student understanding. You might take some higher-achievers away from the lesson in which this is introduced, and ask them in a group to come up with an eight-step road that an individual might follow to reduce the unsatisfactoriness of life: what eight things in life could a person do if they wanted the world to feel less pain?

Give them just ten or fifteen minutes to do a poster/ whiteboard slide of their eight, while the rest of the class get on with the learning. Ask the group to tell the class about their 'path'. Point out that the Buddha was good at this – your students will not have 500 million followers in 2500 years time (unlikely!). Ask the rest of the class to comment on the 'path' the students have suggested, and send them away again to revise it in the light of their learning from the Buddha's Noble Eightfold Path.

Aung San Suu Kyi: Buddhism and politics

From pp.25-30, students will learn the story of two dilemmas that shaped the life of Nobel prize winner Aung San Suu Kyi. Ask students to check where she currently lives and what she does. In 2012, as this book is published, she is touring Europe to pursue justice and rights for her people.

Lat Blaylock, who wrote these pages, sent them to a Buddhist friend to comment. He liked the work, but he said 'The generals who imprisoned her – of course they were Buddhists too.' In many religions, there are inspiring followers and great souls – but there are worrying examples of how religion doesn't seem to make people good.

- Ask students to explain in as many ways as they can why religious practice can lead to great good, but does not do so for everyone.

- Film review: set two students the task to review *The Lady*. It's the DVD biopic of Aung San Suu Kyi's life. They should imagine writing a review for the 'Buddhist Bulletin' (an imaginary British magazine read by British Buddhists) and for 'Rangoon Times' (an imaginary Burmese newspaper sympathetic to the generals). How would the two reviews differ?